99

psalms

99

psalms

SAID

Translated from the German by
Mark S. Burrows

PARACLETE PRESS
BREWSTER, MASSACHUSETTS

2013 First Printing
99 Psalms: SAID

Copyright © 2013 Preface, Afterword, and English translation by Mark S. Burrows

ISBN: 978-1-61261-294-2
Originally published in Germany as SAID, *Psalmen* Copyright
© 2007 Verlag C.H. Beck oHG, Munich.

Library of Congress Cataloging-in-Publication Data

Said, 1947-
  [Poems. Selections. English]
  99 psalms / Said ; translated from the German with a preface and afterword by Mark S. Burrows.
      pages cm
  "Originally published in Germany as SAID, Psalmen (Munich: C. H. Beck, 2008)"—Title page verso.
  Includes bibliographical references.
  ISBN 978-1-61261-294-2 (pbk.)
  I. Burrows, Mark S., 1955- II. Title. III. Title: Ninety-nine psalms.
  PT2679.A3355A2 2013
  831'.92–dc23   2013007310

10 9 8 7 6 5 4 3 2 1

Published by Paraclete Press
Brewster, Massachusetts
www.paracletepress.com
Printed in the United States of America

for my parents

Robert and Marion Burrows

with abiding gratitude

look

i attend to things

with their quietly flowing creed

SAID

Contents

Acknowledgments   *ix*

Preface   1

Psalms   15

Notes on the Psalms   117

Afterword   119

Acknowledgments

Five of these poems first appeared in the translation issue of *Poetry* 199 (March 2012); four also appeared in *Seminary Ridge Review* 16 (Spring 2013).

Preface

The poems we need are often those that refuse to leave us unattended. They come to question and to comfort, to clarify and disturb, seeking in their own way to touch our lives and perhaps even to change us. They offer themselves as illuminations of a sort, casting their light into the shadows that cling to us and gesturing toward a path we might follow through the trials that beset us along the way.

Again and again, such poems startle us in our certainties as in our complacence. They remind us to look beyond what we know, or think we know, and, as the author of these psalms puts it, to "believe in truths / that expand beyond the field of our vision." [11][1] They assure us when we stumble in our doubt that "only seekers see," [73] inviting us to embrace the whole of our lives, including our disappointments and failings, as beginnings of a new path. "[L]et us touch the darkness and / the torn flesh of love," [69] the poet suggests, finding our way to a form of prayer that is "like a river / between two shores," seeking "new skin / that can bear this world." [43] Poems of this sort activate what another poet has called "the acute intelligence of the imagination," a transformative power representing "the sum of our faculties."[2]

These psalms engage us with such an imaginative intelligence. In their unique way they bear witness to the heart's descent into loneliness and despair, and gesture to the ascents we also know in moments of compassion and generosity. They speak words that unsettle our firmly held conventions, calling for "the strength to ponder and clarify" our lives. [53] They ask for what the poet calls "a wordless space close by" [52] so that we might make room in our lives for new ways of thinking and living. In such ways these late-modern psalms, like their ancient Hebrew antecedents, turn us with fierce honesty and authenticity toward the often difficult realities we face in our lives. They beckon us to come forth from the tombs of our grief, and rebuke us when we linger in the valleys of self-pity or resignation. Above all, they invite us to discover our own voice—and our own "self"—as we read them slowly, "chewing" their language to recall an image often found in ancient monastic literature, line by line, image by image, and even word by word. They open something within us, slowly and steadily, that can only be found in such a slow reading, leading to the insights and puzzlements we discover by means of "an incandescence of the intelligence," one that "rescues all of us from what we have called absolute fact."[3]

When I first encountered these psalms in their original German, they seemed intimately familiar to me, though I'd not known of them before then. Nor had I ever met their author, the contemporary poet who goes by the pen name SAID, an Iranian who emigrated to Germany as an engineering student in the late 1960s—but eventually gave up these studies to pursue a writing career; I tell the story of my discovery of SAID's work in the Afterword to this volume.

When I first heard the poet reading several of these psalms, some of the lines ignited that rush of energy that comes in moments of unexpected insight, while others touched a deep sensibility within me through the intimate tenderness of their language. What drew me to them from the start was the power of their allurement, and their witness to truths we can only come to know in and through our embodied lives. In such ways they seemed remarkably like some of the Hebrew Psalms, though their thought-world is unmistakably modern, even late-modern, and thus often a distant echo of the cadences of their biblical predecessors.

Over the years since, the poems found in this strange and wonderful new psalter have become trusted companions on my journey. I hope they might become such a presence for you as well. If so, they will not come offering advice or promising answers to life's great questions. They will be more like the deep "stirrings" that unsettle us, that move us in the silent depths of our being, that "place" within us that is "boundary and center at once," [28] as SAID puts it. But this will mean facing the anguish we know in our bodied lives and learning to "believe in the flesh / its extravagance and its incorrigibility." [68] Such an experience is no small gift, even if often a discomforting one. Nor will it be unfamiliar to those who have heard the cry in our own lives that resounds in the ancient Psalter:

> Deep calls to deep
>> at the thunder of your cataracts;
> all your waves and your billows
>> have gone over me. (Ps. 42:7)

Or, in the echo one hears in one of SAID's psalms:

> lord
> burn
> so that your light divides us
> because i seek refuge with you
> from my truths [77]

As you can see, these poems are distinctly—one might say peculiarly—modern in diction and voice. Yet if the function of psalms is to remind us of the complexities we face in our lives without offering answers, then SAID's psalms are not unconventional at all. Like the "wild wood dove" of Gerard Manley Hopkins's "Peace," SAID's psalter "comes with work to do, he does not come to coo, / He comes to brood and sit." This should be stated plainly at the outset as a kind of "consumer warning," since many who turn to the biblical Psalms select the sweet and lovely ones and ignore or avoid the others—though these are probably the ones we need the most. Why? Because they insist on naming the often difficult story we encounter day by day in our lives, the one we face with all its duplicities in the shadows of our own hearts. A selective approach that would avoid such dark recesses, whether driven by fear or wishful thinking, is finally enervating because untrue—and thus unable to take account of the full range of our humanness.

A word of caution, then, at the outset: these new psalms have something of the sharp and rough edge felt in the rhetoric of the ancient Hebrew Psalter. They occasionally offer soothing words of comfort, but more often bring a measure of the prophet's stinging critique—aimed first of all at the psalmist's own "tribe." None of these poems would ever be chosen to grace a modern greeting card, the kind featuring soft pastel backgrounds, luxurious floral bouquets, or idyllic sunsets over quiet harbors. No, these are psalms for a deeper and more rugged journey, one that faces the deceptions and despairs of our hearts and exposes the hypocrisy choking our public life. For this reason, they are the psalms we most need today, warning us against the dangers of "the songs of our solemn assemblies," in the thundering words of the prophet Amos, as well as the banalities of misguided piety.

SAID speaks courageously against the empty moralism so dominant in our culture. He turns a fearless voice against the deceit of those who judge others for the weaknesses they refuse to acknowledge in themselves—those blinding "shadows" of the psyche, in the language of psychoanalysis. He exposes the abuse of power and privilege, avoiding every trace of sentimentality and turning from the seduction of what Dietrich Bonhoeffer called "cheap grace." These poems offer a distinctively late-modern answer to the question posed by Jesus's first disciples, "Lord, teach us to pray," and they dare to do so while at the same time facing the complexities of modern pluralistic societies as well as the inequities sponsored by a globalized economy. In such ways, SAID, addressing God, speaks a word in defense of those oppressed by others who "have retreated / after devouring me until they hungered no more," such that "what's left is a legion of hecklers / who take shelter behind your façade." [24] A psalm like this reminds us that mercy, that most necessary of virtues, is most needed when it is not deserved. Those who have faced the fire of condemnation and survived know what SAID is speaking about; it is for them, first of all, that these psalms speak.

I am grateful to bring SAID's voice to English readers, since it is one that helps us make sense of what it means to live with passion and integrity in such times as these. They plead for the renewal that is always close to us:

> lord
>
> give me new skin
>
> and don't ignore the murmuring of my flesh
> [79]

There is another power to SAID's verse. These psalms voice a yearning for an embodied spirituality that is able to move us beyond the often narrowing boundaries of institutional religion. Simply put, SAID offers an authentic way of praying, one that is direct and unsentimental, both simple and demanding enough to voice a hope that can move us.

Yet it is just as true that these poems find their grounding in the three Abrahamic religious traditions, and surely this is another source of their allure. The choice of writing ninety-nine psalms will echo for Muslim readers the ancient tradition that Allah is known by precisely this number of names, while one—"the last / the hidden" [1]—remains ultimately beyond us and thus unknowable. Similarly, the story of Cain and Abel [95] finds a place here in a form reminiscent of the interpretive freedom of rabbinic midrash and its retelling in the Qur'an. Furthermore, the address to the "lord" found in these poems carries a sense of both the intimacy and the distance found in the biblical Psalms, an ambivalence SAID renders in the language of longing heard throughout his psalter. And yet readers from these religious communities will be joined by many others outside their boundaries who also find themselves overcome by "a great sorrow," whom "the word has overpowered," and yet also know to "keep still" in order to learn how to love again. [89]

We need psalms like these in our day, psalms that can stir us like a cool night wind across a parched desert or a gentle rain after a long drought. We need poems that are perceptive and audacious enough to call upon the "lord" to "listen within [our] solitude" and "stand by those too / who stay and wait" for his coming. [10] What might we come to know if we dared to ask the "lord," with the poet, to "bear / the brokenness / of [our] body" and not "confuse revenge with justice"? [20] And what could we discover if we followed his lead in asking for "new skin" to touch and feel this world with a child's wonder rather than an adult's worry? We also need a psalter that does not wait for some "still, small voice" but rather calls directly upon the "lord" to

be loud and urgent
share in my life and my passions
accompany me

> all the way to your bread
>
> so that my word might wake [22]

Poems like these encourage us in facing the hungers we feel in our lives, while also promising to lead us to the nourishment we long for, that "new language" [47] we need when we find ourselves silent—or silenced. This collection, *99 Psalms*, is suited for our times, giving us poems that speak a "word out of the silence" and provide "light out of the darkness."

$\sim$

I am glad to acknowledge my gratitude to those whose assistance was indispensable over the last year, while I completed work on this translation. First and foremost, my thanks go to SAID for his generosity in inviting me to create what he called from the start "our psalms." His encouragement over the years and the friendship that has grown in the process have been an unexpected gift; indeed, this collaboration could well stand in answer to the Romantic poet Hölderlin's brooding question, "What use are poets in destitute times?" From the beginnings of this project several years ago, the assistance of others has shaped this book for the better. I am particularly fortunate to have had Jon M. Sweeney as my editor once again. Jon immediately recognized the value of this book when I shared the idea of it with him in a

San Francisco diner in 2011. Since that time, he has generally trusted—and often improved—my work as a translator and poet; the journey SAID's *Psalmen* took in finding their "second life" in my translation has much to do with Jon's editorial instincts and artistic sensibilities. It also reflects the high standards of his colleagues at Paraclete Press, Sister Mercy Minor and Sister Madeleine Cleverly, whose able stewardship of this project exemplifies all that is noble in the still venerable but increasingly fragile publishing business.

Others have offered vital encouragement and affection along the way. Among them I am glad to thank those most intimately involved in my life during the year when I completed this book: my spouse, Ute Molitor, who talked through many of the translation challenges these psalms presented, and stood by me—a favorite phrase of SAID's in these psalms—in ways that exceed what words can say; my daughters, Emma and Madeline, constant sources of love in our lives, whose commitments to bring about positive change in our world emulate the rose which knows "to bare itself / and shine by day" [96]; my parents, Robert and Marion Burrows, and my brothers, David and John, who have always embodied the truth for me—and never more generously than during the past years—that "love is as strong as death" (Song of Songs 8:6).

I am also pleased to thank Chris Wiman, who believed in these poems and my translations of them from the start, and whose own poems—particularly those in his recent volume *Every Riven Thing*—have offered glimpses of a gritty beauty hewn from the heart of suffering when I needed them most. I am also grateful, finally, for the circle of friends whose unswerving love and support over the last year have been a gift of saving grace, above all John Ohlson, Ulrich Wippermann, Mary Catherine Bateson, Carl Scovel, Robert Jonas, and John Haule. Each knows the depth of my gratitude for the ways they embody what it means to "wait for a new light" [78] and thus tend the precious gift of friendship.

Those who write know that this work, shaped in the matrix of solitude, depends on this gift above all others. I am glad to dedicate this volume to these colleagues, family members, and friends who stand among the circle of all who still "believe in beauty" [48] and know to

. . . watch over your word

so that love be found anew

and we win back our wildness [4]

This work bears a deep measure of their affection, and is a sign of my gratitude. These psalms are theirs as well.

MARK S. BURROWS

Albuquerque, New Mexico

1 SAID, *Psalmen* (Munich: C. H. Beck Verlag, 2007), 75; all citations noted in brackets are from SAID's poems as translated and numbered in this volume. In the original German volume, they are not noted by number; since they begin on p. 7, and are never more than a single page in length, one can find the original by adding six to the numbers noted here in brackets.

2 Wallace Stevens, "The Figure of the Youth as Virile Poet," in *The Necessary Angel,* in Wallace Stevens, *Collected Poetry and Prose* (New York: Library of America, 1997), 681.

3 Ibid., 680–81.

"for I am freeing you from cruel gods,
and we're going to a god who belongs to us"

—GABRIELA MISTRAL

psalms

[1]

lord
you can pray to everything
that is near me
because i've given up my claim on
any privilege
so that i won't be immobilized by my own light
and i ask you o lord
reveal all your names to me
even the last
the hidden

[2]

lord
make room
for the rebellious one i am
for my angerless hands
for my selective loyalty
that betrays everything
except dreams and prayers

[3]

lord

let us take up the conversation again

after the long enforced silence

that came after you undid your creatures

in auschwitz

in hiroshima

in halabtsche

in srebrenica

do you fall to your knees before the sacrificed?

and before the perpetrators as well?

and do you believe

that we can survive the temptation of an even more
    radical love

without your word?

[4]

look o lord
i don't sing your praises
but i seek you
with my limbs
which i've tamed just for you
for i want to keep watch over your word
so that love be found anew
and we win back our wildness

[5]

lord
let me be a water puddle
that mirrors your heavens
and murmurs your prayers
so that the cicadas might understand me
show yourself o lord
even if you have no other choice
than to come in the fierce coursing of blood
and take in the refugees
because every fleeing ends in your eye
even if those who flee forget you in their time of
    need
because only those who doubt in you
seek you

[6]

lord
appear nakedly with bread
and destroy the colors
so that we might never again go astray
but show yourself to us
before supermarkets sell you dirt cheap
on their bargain tables
and cell phones mutate into gods
appear as a lawless illiterate one
remain without light and vulnerable to seduction
but hurry
because even the wind deprives us of the deceit

[7]

lord
hurry and mingle time with space
so that the madness might come to an end
teach us the tiger's humility
in submitting to the moon by night
and the lion's courage
in savoring his digestion
without idly tearing his prey apart
and the donkey's wisdom
in coolly bearing the stranger's burden
without losing his bearing
and grant us the aster's simplicity
in delighting in each spring's arrival
without giving a thought to the fall with its greedy
    fingers

[8]

lord
wait a little while
before you wager a new creation
and this time make more animals and plants
so that we might survive as vanquished ones
prevent us
from penetrating the carnation's mystery
because we're incapable
of being content with such knowledge
but unite us with the grass of the plains
with the sea's surf
and smile upon our thirst for perfection
because this is not worthy of you

[9]

lord
consider the blind worm and the rain-worm
when pride overcomes you
consider too the daffodil
and reconcile it to its puddle
smile
so that your justice might become more bearable
withstand my dreams
without forgetting my mother
ponder this o lord
that you're nothing without our bodies
so watch over our skin our sweat our waste
so that in your loneliness you
won't be hardened like a church

[10]

lord
spread wide your arms
and protect us
from the multitude of your guardians
stand by those who wander
who've not lost the gift of hearing
and listen within their solitude
stand by those too
who stay and wait for you

[11]

lord
despair of us
because we've become so confident
with our calculations and our machines
and have unlearned doubt
let us believe in truths
that expand beyond the field of our vision
because every number eventually bears
a Moloch
that in time will devour us

[12]

lord
attend to your name
which i invented for you
it derives from the inner life of things
and should burrow into our gut
give your light to lovers
because they have no other
see how their eyes shine
when they deny you and the world
help them o lord
grant hearing to them and to their bodies
so that you might continue to learn from your
    creatures
bless the sweat of their bodies
and the spit of their mouths

[13]

lord
pray
pray aloud against the clamor of the human hand
that seeks to drown you out
and come on quiet soles
so that we might attend to your footsteps
strive
to acknowledge our prayers
even when they appear in some other guise
for no prayer ever unbinds itself from its origins
with the one who prays

[14]

lord
take up the speech
by which i pray to you
grant me the gestures
that have grown within me in your absence
that i might remain true to my incorrigible nature
and take up your weakness

[15]

lord
stand by my friends
so that they might bear with me
without renouncing me
so that they might love me on account of my
    weaknesses
and warn me
when i feel strong
and stand by them
so that they might distinguish the one from the
    other

[16]

lord
attend to your word
so that my word might flourish
through me and beyond
and seek the wind for us
that binds the north with the south

[17]

lord
understand
i don't want to be subdued
not by the word not by the sword
so let
me love myself
so that i might remain devoted to you
and don't fear my word
when it seeks to bind you to me

[18]

it's about time o lord
that you renounce vengeance
to save our memory
so proclaim
that purity isn't the sister of truth
and respect at last my winter-lies
give pardon o lord
because the human is an unwarmed being

[19]

look lord
where your name once dwelt
ravenous ones now live
who no longer hunger
and know no ways of their own
because they chase after things
that they can merely possess
their vanity eats the earth bare
and fails to recognize your voice

[20]

lord
stand by me
bear
the brokenness
of my body
before i ban it from my tongue
and help me resist
the establishment and its doings
but stand by me
so that i don't confuse revenge with justice
and let me never take the former into my hands

[21]

lord
agree with me
that each body is holy
with all its passions
and that two bodies embracing never defile
     themselves
and stand by me
so that i remain part of this stirring
in order to draw closer to you

[22]

lord
keep on wandering forever and never
settle down
because no dwelling places remain
only footsteps
be loud and urgent
share in my life and my passions
accompany me
all the way to your bread
so that my word might wake

[23]

lord
don't bother me
with your prayers and precepts
remain mute within earshot
and fight with me against exhausted reason
and for a beauty
that also transcends this boundary

[24]

look o lord
my enemies have retreated
after devouring me until they hungered no more
what's left is a legion of hecklers
who take shelter behind your façade
make for me new enemies with a unique
     language
lord
my friends have forgotten to die
and lose their way
so help me o lord
to remain provisional
so that my sorrow doesn't lose its beat

[25]

lord
stay with me
even when i nourish myself from ashes and salt
be still and listen to each of the names
i lend you
for i want to distinguish you from the false gods
give me patience to endure the vain
with their empty words
and the converts
who strive to confirm their opposite
and make
my waiting full of revolt

[26]

lord
when you appear
destroy the calendar
disguise yourself
and appear as a seduction
to test our capacity for suffering
give me the strength
to distinguish the blinded from the blind
so that i might be unjust to none of them
and let there be room for fleeing between us
so that this love might endure

[27]

look at the passersby o lord
who stroll right past the beggar
which puzzle do they want to pose for you?
pray to us
be reconciled with our failings
because only on account of them will we become
    beautiful
and consider this
it is our light
that gnaws away at you

[28]

look o lord
i move toward you
without addressing you
because the word holds within itself the danger
of conscience shifting between us
so respect my silence
which is boundary and center at once
a ford crossing over to you
it saves me from the abyss within me
which is so near
that it remains invisible and dazzles

[29]

look lord
i go to a tree and kiss its trunk
out of respect for its age and accomplishment
and i pray to you
without seeking for proof of your existence
in my little cottage shines a simple light
at night i go out
and lay myself on the earth
without fear without demand

[30]

lord
let me be open with you
your nakedness will find something
with which to cover itself
look lord
i convey my sorrow to each ant
i step on
and my joy to each cloud
i don't touch
and i don't allow myself to be duped by you
my prayer searches for you and leads me onward

[31]

lord
when you arrive
we'll be light
bread and water
the table is set and the door ajar
come and be seated among us
free me of the belief
that you're only faithful from a distance
and speak with me
in the unharried speech of animals
who watch us from afar
with their unadulterated hunger

[32]

lord
praise me
because i've endured much
without a single sign from you
perhaps you're only the echo of my cry
if so help me
make a song of my lament
with which approaching strangers might warm
    themselves

[33]

don't be afraid
o lord
of my heart
with its intemperance
praise the barefooted
when they shine with their lies
it's their only shelter
be shade for the one
who sees you
and sun for the one
who seeks you

[34]

lord
call your angels with their rattling pride
back to heaven
and leave crumbs of bread on the earth for us
look lord
i'll praise you
until you're on the earth
close to me and to the grass
look
the rose also prays and waits

[35]

lord
pray
that we recognize you
when you come
destroy the go-between gods
with their grand airs and their daily needs
set your seal upon your houses
and don't be afraid of our nakedness
let the cypresses be your messengers
for they stand upright and whisper
and don't try to convert the wind

[36]

look lord
i'm the one moving
you need only to remain steadfast
keep silent
so that you hear me
and the voices of others
which have become quieter in your absence
lord
i know nothing about you
yet am full of longing
i only want
you to believe in me
though you know everything about me

[37]

lord
guard my freedom
even when it seeks to displace you
and consider this
it isn't the light and its refractions
that suppress you
but rather the shadows of your absence
so stand by me
when i extend my limbs
and become a traitor
i only want to find my own path
that leads to you

[38]

lord
rip them apart
those membranes between us
made of breath and lies
let me be loud and overbearing in my prayer
so that you wake up and
attend to my desires
for i want to watch your work
without falsity without regard

[39]

lord
believe in my word
otherwise we'll never find each other
and stand by me
when i utter your name
just as you stand by the young chick
slipping out of the egg
so that it might believe in you

[40]

lord
i don't want to distinguish
the creator-god from the redeemer-god
in exchange for this promise
to make no distinction
between god-fearers and god-seekers
and be done with the pious
who stand in our way
because they stress only what divides
receive my prayer each day
which i silently address to beauty

[41]

lord
stand by me and by my simplicity
which leads me to you
because i want to grasp the earth's trustworthiness
don't be an escape o lord
but rather a companion
on paths to come

[42]

lord
don't demand of me
that i reach you
by the circuitous path of sin
perhaps these chasms of mine that lead me to
    your feet
are enough for us
and behold the birds
that fly up to the sky because of the stone the
    children threw
as if they were striving
to bring me closer to you

[43]

lord
i refuse
to engage prayer as a weapon
i wish it to be like a river
between two shores
for i seek neither punishment nor grace
but rather new skin
that can bear this world

[44]

lord
save me from the gods who never weep
who quickly manage without me
look
i have no fear
but i do feel dizzy
i obey the course of things
until i've captured them both
light and moths

[45]

lord
you're no house
before which death loiters
no window
through which i watch the world
no door
through which i enter
perhaps you're a pebble
that i always carry in my pocket
look o lord
i'm close to you

[46]

lord
i believe in the disorder of things
and in a god
who doesn't infect us with his reason
who also endures the stillness
without prayer or candle
don't doubt my hands
o lord
for they press each thing that's beautiful
until they grasp you

[47]

lord
come back to me
and make a new language
because i refuse
to choose between you and my passions
and won't believe in freedom after death
only to come to know you
give to me o lord
a new freedom
eloquent and without death

[48]

lord
give me new feet
so that i neither creak
nor trample on anyone
and praise you solely with my gait
because
when i believe in beauty
i need a prudent god
who trusts me with his mystery

[49]

lord
now and then i need your absence
create a mediating god for me without words
who listens to me
until i gain the strength
to belong to something other than a minority
and lose the belief
that a majority can help when facing the darkness
and give me the equanimity
to bear my exile
this long sleeplessness
that seeks to reconcile me to my death

[50]

lord
dwell within my stillness
until you and i
decipher the demeanor of the outcasts
attend to me o lord
until the tides bring in a new truth
rhythmic and strange
until we're blind enough
for spume and mussel
and deaf enough
for wind and gulls

[51]

lord
i know
i'm only a messenger
let me unlock my message
without straying from my path
and leave a question behind
bind me to my times
from which i've escaped
and help this age
to endure me again

[52]

lord
i don't want a ravenous wolf
or a soft pillow
but only a clearing
look
i'm sitting in the shadow of your tales
and persevere
don't fear me
or my bold wishes
grant me a space between
a wordless space close by

[53]

lord
give me the strength to ponder and clarify
for i seek you
with my flesh with my sorrow
and when you return from abroad
with a tattered memory
then speak
i beg you o lord
in the language of mothers
who wait for their children

[54]

lord
grant that i remain incorrigible
protect me from an accommodating reason
with its postmodern furies
so that i might not lose my excitability
for then i would also lose you
listen to me
o lord
not to those
who listen to you
for they speak
with a blend of god and reason
useful and adaptable

[55]

lord
remain a stone of contentedness
blindly thrown into the ranks of subordinates
such that the hangover of reason
might not win over the intelligence of the
    indifferent
and save me
o lord
from rounded-up facts
from all too sensible friends
and from fearless enemies

[56]

banish
o lord
the prophets of the day
who only want to tame me
abolish the laws
the blunt handiwork of the sated
and lead me into a place
that soothes my brokenness
that listens to me
without demanding loyalty

[57]

grant me
o lord
a beautiful death
deafening and blind
which won't distort my vision
disguised and seductive as it is
without betraying its name

[58]

look o lord
i'm ready for my journey
and haven't unlearned whispering
let me grasp the link
between the torturer and the tortured
so that the place of arriving might change
because of my fleeing
and pray for me
that the houses which i abandoned
might not harden themselves

[59]

lord
make me invulnerable
to laughter from the outside
and cravings from within
so that I can live peacefully
amid the rumors
that are peddled about
and give me strength
not to misjudge the mortar of lies

[60]

look o lord
i don't separate good from evil
i want to resist them both
so strengthen my loins
so that i might know the flesh of my beloved
and thus praise you
just as her flesh
grasps your glory too
and take my laughter from me
whenever it triumphs

[61]

lord
grant
that my word
borne of darkness
might tempt you
and stand by me
that i never lose my hunger
and make my exile one I could always lose
as well as my homeland

[62]

lord
support me
in my plots
against sober gods
with their meager warmth
let me never arrive
for every stranger
is a messenger from the land
he left behind

[63]

lord
give me hearing
for i want to attend to the prayers of others
even if they wound my eyes
see to it
that i remain barefoot and
listen to my own steps
don't let me live beyond my times
and let me die
before pride blinds me

[64]

lord
when you appear
bring along the animal
that matches my longings
with its naked bestiality
its greedy claws
and its bleary eyes

[65]

lord
give your voice to the silenced
for then rebellion
might grow from their gaze
and grant
that i lend form to this urge
so that i might grasp the tumult of the spray
and the perseverance of the leaves of grass

[66]

lord
let us be lovers
even if our knowing grows
and reduces the truth
look o lord
both the heathen and missionaries fall into the grass
and grow no more
angels run about on the metal window ledge
proud of their uselessness
and proclaim new gods

[67]

lord
when you're far from me and forsaken
will you keep silent then?
will you conceal my name?
look lord
you and i
we're one truth
when we whisper with each other
we'll be a bridge
for the feet of lovers

[68]

lord
i believe in the flesh
its extravagance and its incorrigibility
and when i wake your empty place
with this talk
then i'm filled with hope
that our conversation might become a prayer
for the lonely

[69]

look o lord
human beings can pound a hole in a wall
and pray to it
so let us touch the darkness and
the torn flesh of love
do i have to ask each and every day
whether it receives its light from your hand
or does it suffice
for me to savor the day and its light?

[70]

lord
stand by me
that i not fear death
but rather find in its path something of the quiet
that was withheld from me in life
and grant that this quiet
might shape the course of my daily work

[71]

lord
let me live in harmony with my guts
because i can't get by either with god
or with reason
i need an unreal form of the real
to seize the offenses of my soul
so appear o lord
in a flock of birds
so that it takes me a long time
to pluck you from the crowd

[72]

lord
when i grasped the rotting of the arbor
and its desire
not to evade the tide
i sought a conversation with you
because i want to see through the darkness
and the capacity of your light
look
i attend to things
with their quietly flowing creed

[73]

lord
how many numbers do i still need to learn
until you arrive?
look
i'm not waiting
i'm praying
so let me be both
citizen and wanderer
one seeking and one sought
because only seekers see
and only the sought find

[74]

i don't pray only to you o lord
but also to the wind and plain
because i want
to lessen the gap between you and nature
so that you might bear the weight of my words
look
my word eavesdrops on stones
in seeking to find a way to you
so keep silent and listen to the gait of my speech
which submits to your silence

[75]

lord
do you want to remain the eternally unavailable
    one?
or do you grow with my prayer?
then reveal yourself also to the beggar
beneath the undivided heavens
and to the stray mare under the shelter
be path be night
until walking in the light i fall into the snare

[76]

look lord
i draw near like a defenseless continent
that wants to be neither conquered nor caressed
my kiss should bind these
the eagle with the worm
for i eat the bread of the earth
and judge the work of the day
my prayer wants to step forth from speech
and disturb your solitude
for this i bear on my tongue
my wings and my abysses

[77]

lord
be silent!
even if my speech seems arrogant to you
look
i'm an unassuming individual
until i become one with the light
and i want to share everything with you
even the fissures of my prayer
for the broken light terrifies me no more
than the long shadow of my deeds
lord
burn
so that your light divides us
because i seek refuge in you
from my truths

[78]

someone must pray for us
o lord
so that the curse of empty prayers might cease
let us wait for a new light
afterward you could even appear in the form
of a marble
then the truth and the lie break against your
transparency
and thus you would be a gentle animal
before whose mouth the zealots fall silent

[79]

lord
before reason breaks forth
let us seek what is dark
within us
the painful ways of desire
before the errors of civilization blind us
lord
give me new skin
and don't ignore the murmuring of my flesh

[80]

look o lord
i call your name
with the stench rising from the fields
with the pebble calling for the hollow of a hand
aren't we like two pigeons
whom no one entrusted with a message?

[81]

look lord
my humility and my patience
suffice for us
because my flesh acts
in accord with its promises
so make
me obey you
and the unmistakable laws of beauty
so that my brokenness might offset the emptiness
you leave behind

[82]

lord
drive out death
and watch over your creatures
for my intractable hope
believes in the absoluteness of roses
and their continual changes
so conquer o lord
so that we not remain conquered

[83]

lord
i pray to you
to honor my violations
for i know not one of your creatures
that would not have come home to itself through its
    prayer
and let me remain true to the god of childhood
who gives light and comfort
and hears us in that no-man's-land
between arriving and fleeing

[84]

look lord
i've always lived
so that i had something to discard
yet when night falls upon me
i lose faith in the sun
even the undaunted ticks of my pocket watch
can't quiet me
i'm afraid
the darkness falls upon my word
and yet o lord
i want to remain a wound
for my feet
and your eyes

[85]

lord
perhaps i have to pray my way into your timid
    dreams
for you to become a part of me
then i'd grasp the passions of the mint
which fills its seclusion with your name
let me come to recognize my own sufficiency
and understand death as a stage
in order to grasp my freedom

[86]

lord
i seek you
let this search never end
look
they harass me from all sides
the proprietors of god
but they never question their god
because they fear he can't answer
yet i trust in my prayer
in the old arson
who in the search for a new dwelling
betrayed the old houses

[87]

lord
save me from things that aren't symbols
and from words that are symbols for things
make my life quadratic
with clear corners
observe my craving silently
so that your love for me might grow
and let my reason remain provisional
so that by the light of humility
it may reach other planes

[88]

look lord
i don't keep silent
but are you worthy of my word?
perhaps my god sleeps hidden in the grass
keeps silent and watches me
without knowing
if he loves me
when i pray
until you leave your hiding place
and search for my feet

[89]

lord
a great sorrow has come upon me
the word has overpowered me
so teach me to keep still
so that i might begin to love you
and have mercy upon me
for my dwelling is built of memory
i fear the straight line of logic
and lose myself in the body's mystery

[90]

lord
seek me
because i'm obsessed by the wish
to encounter myself in your eye
my prayer is a wager
to understand the ever new place
so save me from the gods
who meddle with numbers and household fetishes
they crawl into every accessible dwelling place
but can no longer console anyone

[91]

lord
my prayers sink beneath the sounds of the day
and yet
they summon all things to prayer
see o lord
i'm burning without needing others of my kind

[92]

lord
i pray
to straddle the abyss
that my language has brought into the world
yet my prayer should
sow no discord
between lovers
and remain as a sounding lead
to measure the depth of my dreams
for i want justice

[93]

lord
call your name loud and clear
for here in this global market
everything is auctioned
that keeps silent
here one strives
to conquer death through increasing
to top happiness with predictability
to number all the clouds
to breed the murmur out of pigeons
to optimize the growth of trees

[94]

look lord
when the angels have saved themselves from your
    anger
they'll put away their eyes and their wings
and then they'll ask each moon
for a god
who is beautiful and opens chasms in the ocean
receives pilgrims soaking wet and
reconciles mulberry trees with fish of the sea

[95]

look lord
abel is still stumbling about
seeking a word of redemption
but whatever he touches
becomes part of the establishment and hassles him
stand by him
until he turns his word against himself
until he surrenders himself
and stand by cain as well
that he not forget his wound and open his eye

[96]

lord
help my word
because it's been fleeing
from my lies for years
help it attain new illusions
so that it might finally understand
that fleeing can also be a dwelling place
look lord
your hands are ready for me
for i don't ask the rose
about the meaning of life
perhaps its task is to bare itself
and shine by day

[97]

lord
watch over the vanquished one
the refuse of his dreams
and the remnants of his speech
for he waits upon another death
and wants to seek the order of things
at the place of their forfeiture
and reveal to me o lord
your hidden name
for the hour
determined by the course of things
and for the moment
when the fact-mongers oppress me

[98]

lord
do i have a right to these prayers?
reduce the collateral damage to other creatures
for i understand myself not as a doer
but as a seeker
like a rain-worm in deep sleep
who has no clue about the big bang and clouds

[99]

lord
do you hear the cry of the masses?
they've found a new god
but even this one knows everything
loves passing humbled through the world
calculates and calls

Notes on the Psalms

[3] These are historical allusions to places that witnessed the horrors of human violence during the twentieth century; see my comment about this poem in the afterword, p. 135–36.

[11] The mention of Moloch (or Molech) refers to an Ammonite god widely worshiped in the ancient Mediterranean world, and often associated with child sacrifice; thus one finds this warning in Leviticus 18:21: "You shall not give any of your offspring to sacrifice them to Molech, and so profane the name of your God: I am the LORD." It also occurs in later literature, coming to stand as an extreme embodiment of evil; Milton berates the destructive power of Moloch in *Paradise Lost* (1667), as does Alan Ginsberg in his celebrated poem "Howl" (1955), where the reference points to an array of urban degradations and the cruel excesses of capitalism. SAID's usage echoes the latter.

[16] SAID's reference to "word" here has the force of the "lord's" way of communicating; thus, he seems to be advising God to take care with the use of language—that is, to consider how such language might be received.

[24] The reference to "enemies" who have "devour[ed]" the psalmist is reminiscent of the dereliction the Hebrew psalmist laments in Ps. 22, with cries for help against the ravaging dogs, the hungry lion, and wild oxen.

[31] The image is reminiscent of the Passover Seder, the meal commemorating the delivery from slavery in Egypt; during that meal, a place is traditionally set at the table and the door to the room left ajar as a reminder of the hope for Elijah's return.

[51] The psalmist here envisions himself in the role Muhammad occupies in Islam as the "messenger" of Allah. Here, however, he seems to be the bearer of the message as well as its interpreter.

[95] This is the single reference to a biblical story, one that is also found in slightly different form in the Qur'an; see Genesis 4 and Qur'an 5:27ff. In SAID's retelling of this story, however, Abel is still alive and has become an instrument of what SAID refers to as the *staat*, which literally means the nation; I have chosen to translate this word as "establishment," a word that first emerged in English during the antigovernment student protest movement in the 1960s and 1970s. SAID's reference, of course, is broader than this, suggesting the state's imposition of power in ways that deny basic freedoms and violate human rights.

Afterword

I first met the author of *Psalmen* in Munich in May 2010. The occasion was the second ecumenical *Kirchentag*, a massive gathering sponsored by the Roman Catholic Church and the Protestant Church of Germany (EKD). This event brought together some 130,000 people for four days of activities—hundreds of lectures and workshops exploring current issues in church and society as well as a dizzying array of theatrical and musical performances imbuing the whole event with the atmosphere of "carnival."

My initial encounter with SAID occurred at a poetry reading held in conjunction with this event, staged in the old city hall on a dreary, rain-soaked night. Despite the weather, an expectant audience assembled in the spacious ceremonial hall, filling every available seat and leaving a large crowd stranded outside in the corridors and stairways. Above us, brightly painted shields ornamented the wooden ceiling, each representing one of the towns or cities of the medieval Bavarian kingdom. Outside in the Marienplatz, a large crowd had assembled for a concert, again despite the weather; the sound of brass and drums was faintly audible within the hall. The massive leaded glass windows that rose from eye level to the top of the vaulted room sparkled from the hundreds of lights strung from poles throughout the square. It was a festive moment, to be sure.

The reading featured contributors to a volume of poems commissioned for this mass event titled *Die Hoffnung fährt schwarz,* which literally means "hope rides black." The phrase borrows a familiar German idiom—*schwarz fahren,* or "riding black"—disparaging those who use public transportation without paying the proper fare; a colloquial English rendering of the metaphor might be something like "hope cheats the system." This description of hope as a "freeloader" would startle most Germans, which was undoubtedly what the organizer of this event and editor of the volume of poems it yielded had in mind. Yet such a claim is no stranger or less suggestive than Emily Dickinson's description of hope as

> . . . the thing with feathers—
> That perches in the soul—
> That sings the tune without the words—
> And never stops—at all—

Both images remind us that hope comes to us without cost and often unexpectedly; each suggests that it violates the rules of decorum, another instance when necessity trumps propriety as the mother of invention. Hope can be edgy, impetuous, even irreverent, somehow finding its way to the soul that desires it.

As the evening progressed, each of the contributing poets came to the stage to read from their work. When SAID's turn came, I noticed that he approached the podium with a thin volume in hand and read half a dozen short poems from what turned out to be his recently published *Psalmen*, or "Psalms."[1] One could sense the audience leaning forward to receive his words, his voice both firm and gentle as he read.

The psalms he chose, like others in this volume, were blunt, vivid, and often startling in their language and imagery. None betrayed any trace of sentimentality. Each took shape in the depths of experience, finding an immediate resonance with the audience. The fierce directness of their language conveyed a marked impatience with intolerance, probing the ambiguities of life with an unflinching honesty in order to remind us—if we had forgotten—that "purity isn't the sister of truth" and asking the "lord" to "give pardon . . . / because the human is an unwarmed being." [18] These are psalms that cry out against the confidence of zealots, with their claims of righteous authority over others—crusaders, campaigners, and jihadists alike.

Though I did not know these psalms and had never met SAID before that evening, his reading struck something deep within me, an experience clearly shared by others in the audience. Particular lines and images settled in my mind as I listened, as if the words were familiar to me though I'd not heard them before. At the conclusion of the reading, I approached SAID to thank him for the reading and asked in the rush of the moment if he would consider my translating several for publication in English. Without hesitating he signed the volume with a stubby pencil he took from his pocket, and gave it to me with a simple word of encouragement. It was the beginning of a collaboration that has led to this publication of what he referred to from the start as "our psalms."

Like the biblical Psalms, those found in this volume allow us to overhear a kind of one-sided conversation with the LORD, one that both reveals what we hold true about ourselves and portrays what we believe about the one we call "God." SAID's choice of lines from the Chilean poet Gabriela Mistral as an epigraph for this collection—"for I am freeing you from cruel gods, / and we're going to a god who belongs to us"[2] —reminds us that our ways of speaking of "God" can mirror our own projections, for better or worse. In this as in any other conversation the language we use to "face" and name the other reveals the shape of our own projections. That is, it tells something important of our own story: through the ways we address the one we call "God" we expose the shape of our fears and hopes, our doubts and convictions, weaving in this mix of sentiment an indivisible strand of experience—which is to say that we are never either righteous or unrighteous, either right or wrong, but rather always an ambivalent mixture of the two. This leads him to ask the "lord" to

> be done with the pious
>
> who stand in our way
>
> because they stress only what divides [40]

At every turn, his psalms speak of a unity deeper than what distinguishes us from each other, a conviction expressed in the psalm in which he asks the "lord" to

> dwell within my stillness
>
> until you and i
>
> decipher the demeanor of the outcasts [50]

His own biography embodies this experience. SAID was born and raised in Iran, and though he initially came to Germany in 1965 to study engineering, he stayed to become a writer—in a language new to him as an adult. Not able to return to Iran because of his opposition to the Shah, he later found himself exiled a second time because of the Islamic Revolution.[3] SAID the psalmist then asks:

> let me remain true to the god of childhood
>
> who gives light and comfort
>
> and hears us in that no-man's-land
>
> between arriving and fleeing [83]

These are poems of exile, psalms arising from a "no-man's-land," prayers imploring the one he names simply as "lord" to "seek the wind for us / that binds the north with the south." [16] They remind us with this metaphor of a hope that reaches beyond religious differences and across the growing disparities between the affluent and the poor—painfully illustrated by the widening chasm separating the so-called developed from the developing nations of these hemispheres. This is a radical political ideal, gesturing toward a sense of the world's essential oneness across our obvious differences. What more vivid metaphor than the wind could one find to speak of a commonality transcending the inequalities of power and poverty that otherwise divide us? As such an image suggests, SAID's psalms are distinctly human in intention and texture, reaching into and beyond the particular traditions of Muslim, Jewish, or Christian prayer. They belong to us, like the ancient Psalms of the Israelite people, as inhabitants of a common "home" on this earth, resident aliens who are willing to resist "the establishment and its doings" [20] when these seek to privilege one nation or people or group over others.

The "god" of SAID's childhood is closer to Rilke's "neighbor God" than to the austere deity often worshiped in religious communities or elaborated in formal theological discourse.[4] SAID addresses this God as *herr*, "lord," the word traditionally used to translate the Hebrew *adonai*.[5] It is a way of addressing the deity across a wide spectrum of religious traditions and cultures. In SAID's hands, though, this "lord" is nothing of an overbearing taskmaster. Rather, he reminds us of a strangely remote and often complicated benefactor who often seems absent to us, but who also stands in need of relationship—at least this psalmist is keen to remind him of this—and thus vulnerable to loneliness and to other emotions we feel.

Given the troubled world we inhabit, one should not expect these psalms to be prayers of ease. In fact, most are not. Like ancient Psalms, SAID's poems find their voice in the face of the anxieties and challenges that beset so many in our world. Unlike many found in the biblical Psalter, however, SAID's tend toward admonition or complaint rather than lament. They often call for resistance to the tides of intolerance and violence that threaten the well-being of the vulnerable among us. Against the din of this madness, he cries out at one point:

> then speak
> i beg you o lord
> in the language of mothers
> who wait for their children [53]

In another, he pleads with the "lord" to

> then reveal yourself also to the beggar
> beneath the undivided heavens
> and to the stray mare under the shelter [75]

These psalms are impatient with the world as it is, refusing any quietism that would accept injustice without protest. As SAID puts it in one of them, "make / my waiting full of revolt." [25] I still hear these words with a measure of the fierce dignity resonant in his voice during that public reading on the windswept night when I first encountered him. The blunt force of direct speech shapes these psalms throughout, inviting us to cry out on behalf of the outcasts, the exiles, and all who suffer. Yet they also speak tenderly at times, mindful of the shadowed places of the heart where consolation is a more immediate need. In the face of such circumstances, these psalms remember how it is that hope "rides black."

How, then, do these poems relate to the genre of biblical Psalms? What attributes, if any, link them to such ancient texts as these that have been prayed across the millennia? Such questions would seem to place a world of difference between the two. SAID, after all, often speaks with a language and tone utterly different from that of the Hebrew psalmists. Nor is it easy to imagine SAID's psalms finding their way comfortably into liturgical settings, whether Jewish or Christian, though the same could have been said of some of the biblical antecedents. And of course, when the more "difficult" Psalms do find their way into the worship of synagogues, churches, and monasteries, they usually do so in a disquieting way. For this reason, it is imaginable that some of SAID's psalms might be included among the prayers of contemporary religious communities, but only if such congregations are courageous enough and wise enough to recognize them as something we most need to hear—and speak—in our day.

But what exactly is the nature of a psalm? Is it a prayer or a poem? Or is it a hymn? In a sense, psalms could be characterized as each of these depending on how and where we experience them. When we find ourselves remembering their phrases in times of private anguish or public celebration, they function as prayer. When we experience them in public worship, joining our voices with others to sing them into being, they serve as hymns. Given the echoes they have stirred in the literature and art of many cultures, they also come to life as poems, spreading their influence beyond the boundaries of religious institutions and their traditions. Could the same be said of SAID's psalms? It seems unlikely that any would ever be used as hymns given the bluntness of their language. But it is surely imaginable that his psalms—offering as poems what Robert Frost once called "a momentary stay against confusion"[6]—might function in the role the Psalter has long played in giving voice to people's fears and hopes.

What is it, then, that has enabled the Hebrew Psalms to endure as they have for thousands of years? Most of all, this is a literature that has been and remains useful in giving expression to a wide range of human emotions, naming both our noblest aspirations and our most lamentable weaknesses. The richness of their metaphorical world and the eloquence with which they voice human experience has assured their persistent use and influence in the three Abrahamic religions, as well as their continuing influence on the broader literary traditions of the West. For many people across a wide spectrum of religious communities and beyond, the Psalms continue to offer what the Protestant reformer John Calvin aptly called "the anatomy of all the parts of the soul": "There is not an emotion of which anyone can be conscious," he insists, "that is not here represented as in a mirror."[7] The breadth of expression they articulate as well as the depths of emotional experiences they plumb allow us to see ourselves from a more complex perspective than we might otherwise know. As a "mirror" in which we see ourselves reflected, they remind us that we must face "all the parts" that make up our experience if we are to know ourselves in spirit and in truth.

Here the contrast between the biblical Psalter and SAID's twenty-first-century psalms comes into sharp relief. Even if the former offer "an anatomy of all the parts of the soul," are they sufficient as models of prayer to give voice to the wonderings and worries of many late-modern people? Or is there some need for new ones to be written? Such questions may seem worrisome to those who understand the Bible as a "closed canon"—that is, a finite collection of authoritative texts that cannot be changed or expanded in any way. After all, they might argue, these Psalms have been regarded as a reliable part of the Scriptures honored by Jews and Christians, and their steady use over many generations by worshiping communities has only deepened their authority. But what are we to make of the admonition voiced repeatedly in these same Psalms to "sing to the Lord a new song"?[8] To ask such questions is not to imply that the biblical Psalms are insufficient. It might suggest, however, that the range of their themes and sensibilities is necessarily limited, at least from our vantage in late modernity.

This is not news to many who have been praying the Hebrew Psalms faithfully across the centuries, as has been particularly true in Christianity's monastic communities. Their members would be the first to remind us that the ancient Psalter is not an infallible guide to the hidden mysteries of the divine, but rather a witness to the altogether fallible ways we live as human beings in the presence of the one we address as "LORD." To this end, they offer us language that we can call upon in times of dire need: "Save me, O God, for the waters have come up to my neck; I sink in deep mire, where there is no foothold; I have come into deep waters, and the flood sweeps over me" (Ps. 69:1–2). They offer ways of naming our fears and hopes in the face of the often tenuous nature of our lives: "As for mortals, their days are like grass; they flourish like a flower of the field; for the wind passes over it, and it is gone. . . . But the steadfast love of the LORD is from everlasting to everlasting on those who fear him" (Ps. 103:15–17). They give voice to the threats we face from those we call our enemies (Ps. 56) as well as the betrayals we experience at the hands of our "friends" (Ps. 55).

They even project onto God the anger we feel in the face of danger, convincing us all too often to call upon the LORD to be vengeful toward those perceived as enemies: "Pour out your indignation upon them, and let your burning anger overtake them. May their camp be a desolation; let no one live in their tents. . . . Let them be blotted out of the book of the living" (Ps. 69:24–25, 28). If mercy is what the ancient psalmists often cry out for, vengeance is what they frequently wish upon those who threaten them. These sentiments are understandable enough. But are they defensible in an age like ours, when the power in our hands could lead to unthinkable levels of destruction? And yet there they are in the Bible. The violent language heard on all sides in the Middle East today reminds us that not much has changed over time. Alas.

Those familiar with the biblical Psalms might well be startled by SAID's collection, but not because they are "new." What is so startling about them—and, I would argue, important—is the ways in which they root themselves in a different source of memory, and lean into a hope utterly opposed to the "law of vengeance," the ancient *lex talionis*.[9] Those who know the ancient story of jealousy and revenge told in Genesis 4, enacted in countless versions through the ages and in every human culture, can but welcome a psalm that modulates this old and familiar narrative in the style of a rabbinic midrash:

> look lord
> abel is still stumbling about
> seeking a word of redemption
> but whatever he touches
> becomes part of the establishment and
>   hassles him
> stand by him
> until he turns his word against himself
> until he surrenders himself
> and stand by cain as well
> that he not forget his wound and open
>   his eye [95]

A poem like this has the capacity to startle us into seeing the "old" story anew by shifting our expectations in radical ways. Such poems prompt us to wonder, "Now why did the poet write that?" and give us the chance to loosen the stranglehold of wounded memories. Why would Abel, the victim in this story, long for "a word of redemption" unless his intent is to unravel the cycle of jealousy and revenge aimed against him—not only for his sake but for Cain's as well? But why would he need to "turn his word against himself" and "surrender himself"? We are not sure, but the claim surprises us, provoking us to return to this ancient story and consider it again from another angle. Puzzlement of this sort works on our unquestioned complacencies. It opens the familiar world we inhabit in ways we—and often enough the poet—could not otherwise have anticipated.

Such poems lure us into the experience of "defamiliarization,"[10] disorienting us and unsettling our worldview. They turn us toward a new field of vision by which we come to view our lives and the lives of others differently. They have what poet Jane Hirshfield describes as a certain "volatility," one that "stems from the inability to hold [the poem's] full meaning in mind."[11] As she goes on to suggest, the "startlement" latent in such poems can "transport us into previously unanticipatable comprehensions."[12] This happens not merely because they are strange, but because they open us unexpectedly to depths of feeling and ways of seeing that touch the hidden world we carry within us. In this manner, too, they remind us of a commonality we share with others, touching upon these vulnerabilities—and above all the wounds we endure as well as those we inflict on others. A psalm like this one—urging the "lord" to "stand by cain . . . / that he not forget his wound and open his eye"— gestures toward something we need to learn in our own experience. It might even startle us in ways quite different from those of the Hebrew Psalter, an interpretive tactic often present in rabbinic literature and Christian commentary alike. SAID's petition, in an earlier psalm from this collection, underscores the importance of such a shift:

> stand by me
> so that i don't
> confuse revenge with justice
> and let me never take the former into my
>   hands [20]

SAID's psalms also consistently address the one he refers to in one of these psalms as "the god of childhood," without any sense that this "lord" is almighty, omnipotent, or any of the other "superpower" attributes associated with God. Unlike the canonical Psalms, these prayers do not presume a privileged relationship to God, and they eschew the "lord/vassal" imagery suggested by such nomenclature. That said, SAID's approach to this "lord" is often peculiar and sometimes awkward, at least when judged from the perspective of the Bible. Sometimes

he portrays his "lord" as one who is somehow depen-
dent upon the poet himself. "[Y]ou're nothing
without our bodies," [9] he insists, and from the open-
ing psalm on repeatedly calls the "lord" to "pray":

> lord
>
> you can pray to everything
>
> that is near me
>
> because i've given up my claim to
>
> any privilege
>
> so that i won't be immobilized by my own
> > light [1]

In a later psalm he goes on in this vein:

> pray
>
> pray aloud against the clamor of the human
> > hand
>
> that seeks to drown you out

and goes on to offer advice to the "lord," as if he were
instructing a child:

> . . . come on quiet soles
>
> so that we might attend to your footsteps [13]

In yet another, he tells his "lord" to

> take up the speech
>
> by which i pray to you [14]

Such a manner of speaking is a world removed
from the petitions and presumptions of the ancient
psalmists. Encouraging the "lord" to pray—*for* us, *in*
us, and even in one of SAID's psalms *to* us [27]—
may strike some readers as arrogant or absurd and

perhaps even as blasphemous. It is surely unorthodox when measured against the overriding tradition of the biblical Psalms. But this means of address has a crucial purpose: it points to the reciprocity between God and humans, between the psalmist and his "lord." It upends our expectations—in this case, vis-à-vis the God we thought we knew, imagining this "lord" as vulnerable, as having a "weakness" we might wish to take upon ourselves—a theme central to Christian reflection on the paradox of the incarnation. [14] It prompts us to wonder who this "lord" really is, and just as importantly, who we are.

Given the fact that we discover much of our identity through the give-and-take of conversation, the dialogical nature of SAID's psalms invite a dimension of self-discovery we might not find in a more direct manner. Could prayer or psalmody be shaped by such an insight? This seems to be the case. One sees this in SAID's reproach of his "lord" for the horrors of human violence when he accuses the "lord" of having "undone"—or, "denatured" them (*denaturieren*)—his creatures, an allusion apparently to the terrible implication that could be—and often is—drawn from an extreme view of divine omnipotence: that is, if God is capable of doing all things and did not prevent such atrocities, God must be somehow responsible for them. SAID goes on to name several places that have witnessed such horrors in recent history—Auschwitz and Hiroshima, Halabtsche and Srebenica—before demanding to know of the "lord": "do you fall to your knees before the sacrificed? / and before the perpetrators as well?" [3]

This is a strange way of speaking, but one we can and probably should imagine if we attribute to God compassion for those who suffer—particularly innocently—and even toward those who inflict that suffering on them. On the basis of such an imagining he asks the "lord" to

> let me grasp the link
>
> between the torturer and the tortured [58]

Such startling claims and queries thrust us into a state of surprise, unsettling our expectations and defamiliarizing us by what Hirshfield calls "the signal of strongly shifted knowledge."[13] One might well say that psalms that fail to do this fail us as psalms.

SAID seems to want to engage us in a kind of dialogue, offering an invitation to a "no holds barred" conversation with God. As he voices this discussion, he posits a radical vulnerability on both sides. The effect, as Hirshfield suggests, is that "each time we enter poetry's realm, we find hunger both wholly present and wholly answered"; in this case, these poems awaken an appetite within us that lures us beyond the narrowing boundaries of "orthodoxy" to give voice to our most intimate longings—regardless of their propriety.[14] That is, they meet our hunger only to intensify it. They remind us that the Psalms, set within other narrative books of the Hebrew Bible, bear witness to the vigorous argument that the human characters in these stories often carried on with their God. Thus, we do well to clarify Israel Abrahams's claim that "in prophecy God speaks to man, and in psalmody man sings to God" to say that such a song, if it is to capture the complex truth of this relationship, must be both temperate and tempestuous, yielding and demanding, intimate and fierce. After all, the partners in this "conversation," if they are to be true to the nature of such an exchange, must be bold as well as vulnerable.

Many of SAID's psalms arise from the situation of exile, recalling the late additions to the Hebrew Psalter (see, for example, Psalm 137). Like his predecessor's "by the waters of Babylon," this contemporary poet knows the pressures of *Einsamkeit*—a word we might render either as "solitude" or "loneliness"—that shape exilic experience, having spent much of his life unable to return to his native Iran. He even suggests that his "lord" knows something of this, [9] perhaps because he must face the mistaken ways in which our projections and confusions render him. For this reason, SAID implores the "lord" to "take in the refugees / because every fleeing ends in your eye," [5] and, pressing in another direction, goes so far as to advise the "lord" to

> . . . keep on wandering forever and never
> settle down
> because no dwelling places remain
> only footsteps [22]

In such ways his psalms articulate anew the aspirations of those who yearn for the familiarities and consolations of their lost homeland. As he puts it early in this collection:

> stand by those who wander
> who've not lost the gift of hearing
> and listen within their solitude
> stand by those too
> who stay and wait for you [10]

SAID reminds us here, as does the ancient Hebrew psalmist forced to live in exile, that those removed from their homeland may have deeper "hearing," a greater attentiveness to such distant things. Solitude or loneliness—that is, *Einsamkeit*—can evoke the capacity of listening and hearing unknown to those who have never left home. *99 Psalms* offers glimpses of this longing rooted in the refugees' yearning for safety, the exiles' desire for welcome, the immigrants' nostalgia for home. In one of the poems, in fact, he reverses our expectations to suggest that it is our work to offer hospitality to this wandering "lord" who also knows a measure of this loneliness:

> lord
> when you arrive

> we'll be light
> bread and water
> the table is set and the door ajar
> come and be seated among us [31]

If exile is the condition shaping many of these psalms, it is no surprise that SAID's "lord" meets us as a fellow wanderer, encountering us in our fleeing, meeting us as a companion who wanders with us on the way. "[F]ree me of the belief / that you're only faithful from a distance," he prays. [31] In the tumble of feelings experienced in his psalms, we find ourselves close to the longings of an earlier poet, Rainer Maria Rilke, who once described the plight of lovers as those who "journey always along the boundaries, one in the other, / having promised each other breadth, hunt, and home"—in other words, lovers who find themselves facing the tensions that belong to the experience of exile, above all the mingled experience of estrangement and intimacy.[15]

As a witness to this sense of uprootedness, SAID repeatedly points to the experience of seeking, yearning, and wandering. The "I" of these poems is restlessly looking for connection, always aware of the absence of what is lost or distant, but driven by a hungering for the taste of an "at-one-ment" in and with the world here and now—precisely as it *is*:

> so let me be both
> citizen and wanderer

> one seeking and one sought
> because only seekers see
> and only the sought find [73]

In another he probes the ambivalence of his quest, calling upon the "lord" to

> . . . stand by me
> that i never lose my hunger
> and make my exile one I could always lose
> as well as my homeland [61]

Just as loneliness awakens a sense of longing for presence, SAID knows that absence can be a valued teacher by awakening us to what is real:

> lord
> now and then i need your absence
> create a mediating god for me without
>   words
> who listens to me
> until i gain the strength
> to belong to something other than a
>   minority [49]

Then, later in the same psalm he petitions the "lord" whose absence he yearns for to

> . . . give me the equanimity
> to bear my exile
> this long sleeplessness
> that seeks to reconcile me to my death

And, in another, he presses this point further:

> lord

> i know nothing about you
> yet am full of longing
> i only want
> you to believe in me
> though you know everything about me [36]

The state of unknowing among those living in exile does more than evoke humility, though it surely does this. It moves them in the direction of mystery, and against those who cling to certainty in order to legitimate their sense of power. One sees this in the opening psalm, where SAID emphasizes what cannot be known, calling upon the "lord" to

> reveal all your names to me
> even the last
> the hidden [1]

This plea recalls the ancient Islamic tradition in which God is known by ninety-nine different names—the exact number of these psalms—but which insists that one name remains unknown and unknowable. This "last" and "hidden" one lies beyond the reach of our knowledge. It is in this sense that we should understand SAID's counterintuitive claim that ". . . only those who doubt in you / seek you." [5] After all, we can only seek what we do not know, and the very act of naming the unknown—and unknowable—is its own form of witness. The mystics and poets remind us that such an "unknowing" lies at the very heart of faith.

Doubt, confusion, and struggle: these are the texture of the psalmist's seeking his "lord" in this psalter, generally prompted by a brooding sense of God's absence. But one can say more than this: this search for the unknowable confronts us with the experience of uncertainty, which is central to the creative life of every artist, inventor, and discoverer. This is a fundamental thread woven through SAID's psalms, and found in the mystical literature of many religious traditions. This sense even presses the poet to address the "lord" and admit that "now and then i need your absence" [49] since distance awakens his longing and seeking deepens his belief. He takes this so far as to confess that "i believe in the disorder of things," [46] a reminder in the larger context of his poems that absence and disorder are a measure of freedom, and this rather than control is the mark of dignity.

Indeed, the freedom found in this absence represents for SAID an inviolable dimension of mystery. Such freedom calls us to approach our lives in the posture of receptivity and reverence, a "not knowing" by which we open ourselves to what is beyond us. Freedom rooted in this kind of vulnerability is indispensable to our capacity for experiencing and expressing hospitality, suggesting that every connection across the distances separating us creates a sense of "home."

What emerges is a validation that knowing can never be exhaustive, that it always includes an "unknowing" within it, reminding us that every true experience of intimacy holds a certain distance within it. We see this when SAID asks the "lord" to

> prevent us
> from penetrating the carnation's mystery
> because we're incapable
> of being content with such knowledge [8]

Our relation to the "here-ness" of things, at least insofar as we honor their essential sanctity, is a kind of knowing that upholds mystery—that allows things to be "other," beyond our control. In this sense, freedom establishes a certain kind of not-knowing or unknowing as essential to our well-being and happiness.

Honoring this essential mystery gestures toward the freedom all things have in themselves, opening us to others, creation, the "lord," and ourselves as well. According to this late-modern psalmist, "faith" as it is sometimes understood and expressed within religious communities too often becomes a means of closure, turning us from the mystery and freedom that belong to the sacred as it is present in others, creation, the "lord," and also ourselves. Thus, he prays:

> lord
> i refuse

> to engage prayer as a weapon
> i wish it to be like a river
> between two shores [43]

The language of these psalms—and one might argue that this holds true for all the language we use—moves instead toward a common destiny between the shores of the "self" and the "other," wherever and however we experience this sacred presence.

In a similar manner the poet describes his prayer as "a wager / to understand the ever new place," [90] an opening of the mind and heart to what is not yet known, or experienced, or even imagined. *Or not yet,* for these poems bring such an imagining close to us as we find ourselves voicing them, and perhaps even rendering them in the cadences of the kind of prayer that seeks the "new" in our lives and in our world. Psalms like these teach us that praying is a form of radical seeing, a bold "revisioning" of old habits and ways that obstruct freedom. As an act of making ourselves vulnerable, prayer is a gesture shaped not by comfort or complaint but rather by an imagining that opens us to the "ever new place" in our lives. Its posture, initiated over and over again in SAID's psalter, arises from the experience of startlement and the call to fight

> . . . against exhausted reason
> and for a beauty
> that also transcends this boundary [23]

For wonder of this kind is what awakens us to the matrix of our creativity. It reminds us of our capacity to change the world we inhabit, encouraging us to live into the freedom that a homeland cannot guarantee and exile cannot take from us. Such praying has everything to do with the shape of our longing. It is a way of attuning ourselves to the world we indwell, a calling upon "the lord" to move among us as a wanderer in the here and now. Above all, it is a quality of attention by which we shape our lives, and thus a way of opening ourselves both to the prophet's critique and to the artist's sense of awe. It is a way of seeking, one shaped by the kind of praise that forms in us—and forms us—not by doing but through patient waiting:

> look lord
> i'll praise you
> until you're on the earth
> near to me and to the grass
> look
> the rose also prays and waits [34]

1 SAID, *Psalmen* (Munich: C. H. Beck Verlag, 2007).

2 I have rendered these lines from SAID's German translation; for an English version, see Gabriela Mistral, "The Flight," in *Gabriela Mistral: A Reader*, trans. Maria Giachetti and ed. Marjorie Agosin (Fredonia, NY: White Pine Press, 1993), 113. It is intriguing that SAID selected the lines of another poet (Mistral) who writes pseudonymously.

3 See SAID's memoir, *Landscapes of a Distant Mother*, trans. Kenneth J. Northcott (Chicago: University of Chicago Press, 2004).

4 For this reference, see my translation in Rainer Maria Rilke, *Prayers of a Young Poet* (Brewster, MA: Paraclete Press, 2013), 40 [6].

5 SAID never uses any capitalization in his poetry or other writings; hence, his use of *herr* in lowercase accords with the way he writes nouns in general, all of which proper German usage would render with an initial capital letter. German usage continues to use *herr* as a formal way of addressing men—e.g., *Herr Braun*—in the way we now use the formal address "mister"—"Mr. Brown."

6 Robert Frost, "The Figure a Poem Makes," in *Collected Poems, Prose, and Plays* (New York: Library of America, 1995), 777.

7 See John Calvin, preface to the *Commentary on the Psalms*, vol. 1, translated from the Latin and collated with the author's French by James Anderson; http://www.ccel.org/ccel/calvin/calcom08.vi.html.

8 See, for example, Pss. 33:3; 96:1; 98:1; and 149:1

9 That is, the "law of retaliation" or retribution. This ancient legal principle is found in the Code of Hammurabi, and later appears in various forms in the Hebrew Scriptures; see, for example, Exodus 21:23–25. Jesus opposed the logic of vengeance; see Matthew 5:38–39, though its persistence can also be seen in the so-called "just war" doctrine and its language about proportionality.

10 The term *defamiliarization* was first coined by Viktor Shklovskij, in 1917, in an essay titled "Art as Device"; he devised this word in order to "distinguish poetic from practical language on the basis of the former's perceptibility." Shklovskij, like many modernist writers, envisioned the purpose of art as preventing an "over-automatization," which causes an individual to "function as though by formula"; see Viktor Shklovskij, "Art as Technique," in *Literary Theory: An Anthology*, ed. Julie Rivkin and Michael Ryan (Malden, MA: Blackwell, 1998), 16.

11 Jane Hirshfield, *Hiddenness, Uncertainty, Surprise: Three Generative Energies of Poetry* (Highgreen, Northumberland: Bloodaxe Books, 2007), 55.

12 Ibid., 45.

13 Ibid.

14 Ibid.

15 These lines are from the Fourth of Rilke's *Duino Elegies*; in Rainer Maria Rilke, *Gedichte 1910–1926*, ed. Manfred Engel and Ulrich Fülleborn (Frankfurt am Main und Leipzig: Insel Verlag, 1996), 211 (my translation).

About Paraclete Press

WHO WE ARE

Paraclete Press is a publisher of books, recordings, and DVDs on Christian spirituality. Our publishing represents a full expression of Christian belief and practice—from Catholic to Evangelical, from Protestant to Orthodox.

We are the publishing arm of the Community of Jesus, an ecumenical monastic community in the Benedictine tradition. As such, we are uniquely positioned in the marketplace without connection to a large corporation and with informal relationships to many branches and denominations of faith.

WHAT WE ARE DOING

Books Paraclete publishes books that show the richness and depth of what it means to be Christian. Although Benedictine spirituality is at the heart of all that we do, we publish books that reflect the Christian experience across many cultures, time periods, and houses of worship. We publish books that nourish the vibrant life of the church and its people—books about spiritual practice, formation, history, ideas, and customs.

We have several different series, including the best-selling Paraclete Essentials and Paraclete Giants series of classic texts in contemporary English; Voices from the Monastery—men and women monastics writing about living a spiritual life today; award-winning poetry; best-selling gift books for children on the occasions of baptism and first communion; and the Active Prayer Series that brings creativity and liveliness to any life of prayer.

Recordings From Gregorian chant to contemporary American choral works, our music recordings celebrate sacred choral music through the centuries. Paraclete distributes the recordings of the internationally acclaimed choir Gloriæ Dei Cantores, praised for their "rapt and fathomless spiritual intensity" by *American Record Guide*, and the Gloriæ Dei Cantores Schola, which specializes in the study and performance of Gregorian chant. Paraclete is also the exclusive North American distributor of the recordings of the Monastic Choir of St. Peter's Abbey in Solesmes, France, long considered to be a leading authority on Gregorian chant.

Videos Our videos offer spiritual help, healing, and biblical guidance for life issues: grief and loss, marriage, forgiveness, anger management, facing death, and spiritual formation.

Learn more about us at our website:
www.paracletepress.com,
or call us toll-free at 1-800-451-5006.

SCAN
TO
READ
MORE

More Important Poetry from Paraclete Press

Prayers of a Young Poet
Translated by Mark S. Burrows

This volume marks the first translation of these prayer-poems into English. Originally written in 1899, Rainer Maria Rilke wrote them upon returning to Germany from his first trip to Russia. His experience of the East shaped him profoundly. He found himself entranced by Orthodox churches and monasteries, above all by the icons that seemed to him like flames glowing in dark spaces. He intended these poems as icons of sorts, gestures that could illumine a way for seekers in the darkness. As Rilke here writes, "I love the dark hours of my being, / for they deepen my senses."

132 pages | ISBN: 978-1-61261-076-4 | $23.99, Hardcover

Astonishments
Selected Poems of Anna Kamieńska

Kamieńska's poems record the struggles of a rational mind with religious faith. Her spiritual quest has resulted in extraordinary poems on Job, other biblical personalities, and victims of the Holocaust. She explores the meaning of loss, grief, and human life. Her poetry expresses a fundamental gratitude for her own existence and that of other human beings as well as for a myriad creatures, including hedgehogs, birds, and "young leaves willing to open up to the sun."

144 pages | ISBN: 978-1-55725-599-0 | $19, Trade paperback